BOOKS BY MARY SWANDER

Poetry

Nonfiction

Heaven-and-Earth House

Heaven-and-Earth House

POEMS BY

Mary Swander

Alfred A. Knopf   New York   1997

The author wishes to thank the editors of the following publications in which these poems first appeared:

Boulevard: "No Wonder"
Crazy Horse: "Muskrat"
The Georgia Review: "Novena"
The Iowa Review: "I-80 Lieder," "Jackpot," "Peelings"
Iowa Woman: "Gulf," "Shunning"
The Kenyon Review: "Amish Phone Booth"
The Laurel Review: "Frog Gig"
The Nation: "Two Skulls"
The New Virginia Review: "Coyote-Fox," "Heaven?"
The New Yorker: "Heaven-and-Earth House"
The Plum Review: "The Art of Acupuncture"
Prairie Schooner: "Mud Road"
Raccoon: "Father Di Pilato at Veteran's Auditorium"
The Rhetoric Review: "On the Orval Yoder Turnpike," "Scheherazade"
River Oak Review: "Rules for School," "Ode to Okra"
The Southwest Review: "Stay Still, Duck"
Tar River Poetry: "Take Two"
Willow Springs: "Early Frost"

The completion of this book was made possible by a fellowship in Creative Writing from the National Endowment for the Arts. The author also wishes to express her appreciation to the Ingram Merrill Foundation and Iowa State University for their support. Special thanks to Robin Behn, Elizabeth Grossman and Michael Rakosi.

For my healing circle, with gratitude

Humans are Heaven and Earth in miniature.

Chinese proverb

Contents

CONTENTS

I

Heaven?

No, it's lying in a field in Iowa
staring at the heavens, stars streaking
the sky, their auras pulsing out, in.
Night of the meteor shower,
night of mosquito netting and pitched tent,
the flap open to the eastern horizon.
Hot, damp, August night when the rooster's crow
folds into its perch and the cricket's song
dives into the same pool as the whippoorwill.
Night of Augustus Caesar and St. Augustine,
Amish date night when the buggies race
home late, their wheels spinning up hill,
lanterns blinking, horses' manes flying.
Pegasus of the tall corn, Pegasus of the fat bean,
under my sleeping bag is the richest earth
on earth, and this is the night of
the Assumption of the Blessed Virgin Mary,
the blessed virgin prairie, the nightcrawlers
floating up through layers of black dirt.
What awaits? A choir of angels,
a chorus of sheep bleating out *how good
is the grass, how good is the flesh.*
How good were the stars to lead me here,
the year of the blue goat, brown duck,
the year of the squawk and coo, the loyal
dog who barked at strange men and storms.
O little town of Kalona, Hannakalona,
Kahlua Kalona, bull town, where the gardens
are ringed in cockscombs and cannas,
and down the road little girls sing hymns

3

outside the window of the dying man
propped with pillows near the screen.
Their voices hover above me, and are gone,
a flock escaped from the barn.
I chase them one way across the ditch,
over the hill, through the neighbor's
orchard and field. I chase them
back toward the house, corner the ram
against the fence, then Aries, Aries
is free and off through the grove
with the ewes and lambs close behind.
So bleat for the ones who never return,
the ones who last just this long,
the empty manger and stall, bleat
for the ones who come again, who ascend
in the clear air, dark night, holy night,
when sounds carry and trails of light
flit over our heads, and bleat for the moon,
the sun, the golden day when we will all lie
down in a field, nothing more to be done.

Amish Phone Booth

The letter of the law is: no lines in from
the outside world. But this phone in a garage
down the road is fine, and a trip across
the field on foot enough to make you think twice
before a call. Above the receiver—chiropractor,

vet, weather report, all numbers penciled
on the wall. Below—a doodle of a stallion
with the caption S T U D. Bareback and buckboard,
they gallop in at night for help with a fire
in Chester Yoder's barn, the hay put up too wet,

or aid with a stuck calf who must be sawed
in half to get out. *Doc, I'm not sure what to do.*
This little room holds in all the pain for miles,
and the joy that doesn't travel by buggy or bonnets
nodding together after church. *The Bontragers*

had another. After thirteen boys, a girl!
After thirteen years, the thin line that runs out
to the transformer still ices, sways in the winter wind,
goes down with any little spring storm.
A person could depend on that thing too much.

More reliable, the fence wire, that runs from
Swander to Yoder to Miller, is never busy,
charges nothing extra, leaves no gap in between.
Better to walk out and tap a message that will
hum from post to post, a party line for everyone

to overhear. Better to ring your alarms out there
in the pasture where the cattle, the sheep,
the nanny goat, their cries bleating across
the grass, will listen, and pass the word.
Please come, and bring the others this time.

Rules for School

From my desk in this old country schoolhouse,
I hear the call of the turkeys
at the farm over the hill. I smell
their fear on the day of the round-up,
the kick in the breast, flush of the wattle,
then dead of a heart attack, and
the other dumb souls mimicking the pain,
until they, too, are still on the ground.
And I imagine all the children together
here in one room, the teacher writing names
on the board to terrify them to their seats.
You, you, and you will haul the water
and wood in. You will clean the latrine.
And I remember the nuns of my youth,
Sister Mary Pilgrim, the one who still
chases me in my dreams, ax and musket wounds.
Here's to you, *ma soeur*, with thanks.
Curtsy and blue blazer, ours was a French order.
And here's to the fun nuns, the novice who
slugged softball home runs, the one
who dug in the garden to plant cabbage,
wiping her hands on her habit,
the one who sneaked a six pack into her cell,
the ones found kissing in the bathroom stall,
the one who fed the ex-cons
in the bread line by the kitchen door
and told stories of the saints,
Lucy thrown into boiling oil, the twelve
North American martyrs de-nailed, de-tongued.
And here's to the tender nuns who swooped

down in their black beads and swept
me up from the playground gravel.
These were friends: Sister Mary Fluff and Feather,
a marvel, the midget nun who sold Tootsie Rolls
and Sacred Heart medals. And the nun
without thumbs who taught us cursive,
Palmer Method, *oval-oval, push-pull and off*.
But most I loved Sister Mary Shaman who
had us singing each morning, *Kyrie eleison*
and the ringing, the ringing of the bells,
a choir of young girls, our heads covered
with veils, the light fanning through
the stained glass, voices in unison rising with
the pipe organ, up, up, up, toward the ceiling,
unsuspecting of what another day was bringing,
how far we'd come and what we had to learn.

School Children

Vernon Miller tells how,
as an older boy,
he had to climb down
into the well pit and
bucket out the snow melt
before it killed the motor.
Bull snakes slithered across
his boot tops and toads
hopped into his cuffs.
He dangled the reptiles
in front of the girls' faces
and chased them across the field.
A person learned to hold it in,
then burst out laughing
at the screams. Such fun,
a guy almost didn't want
to grow up, but remain forever
at a desk here by the window,
staring out, watching himself
at recess sled the pasture hill,
stocking cap pulled down,
a girl's arms wound around
his waist, her fingers
dug in, babushka flapping
in the clear December air.
Oh, the long glide!
The slow trudge back up,
higher and higher,
dragging the rope,
and home in the half-dark—

books in a strap, thermos
in a tin lunch box—
then back and back again,
until he was ten, knew his
continents, his sums,
was big enough to sin, carve
his name in the cellar beam:
VERNON + VELDA.
Vernon Miller tells how
he had to sit and atone
on these back steps.
Door shut, kept away from
his friends, while the rest
of the class went on
with its lessons:
DE-FACE, DIS-PLACE.
They spelled their words
and pledged their lives
to God, a person praying
the rain would keep pouring,
pelting, then the grove
blossom with bloodroot,
violets, and those little
white pantaloons on a line—
Dutchman's breeches.
Vernon hears the rumblings
of the early bumblebees
tapping the nectar,
and suddenly the world
shifts on its huge plates,
the ground cracks,
and down into the cavern
falls everything that's known:
how one and one is two,

how beans follow corn,
how heaven and earth is formed.
In the beginning, ridge
and rift, we were all one,
Pangaean, tongues lapping
over tongues. Now, that's
all undone, but for the rain
that keeps falling,
and soon the whole
school rushing down
the stairs, buckling on
skates, pushing round
and round the tiny basement
roller rink, past the stacks
of boots, coat hooks,
the coal bin, a game of tag,
dip and spin, then Velda,
sweet Velda, smiling,
steadying herself against
the beam, dropping a newt
down his shirt, and flying
off across the floor, the room.

Goatherd's Complaint

When, when, when? Even now your udder
scrapes the ground, teats pouting,
milk dripping, and waddling up the hill,
pelvis wide, joints loose, your burden
bounces with every lift of the hoof.
When, when, when? I built a pen,
hammered the stakes into the dirt,
the post pounder's clank ringing one, two.
Up at three, flashlight shining in the hut,
there you are without a move, a moan, a word,
content to lie on your side, burping cud.
When, when, when? The full moon has come
and gone, the northern lights left their
swirls on so many clear summer nights.
Venus, Jupiter and Saturn have all
fallen in line, and your kid floats down
head first through his own cosmos calling,
come on, come on. But still you resist.
Little she-devil, satyrette, of course
a girl with thorns is mixed-up, but the billy
has already danced—plié, twirl and pirouette.
The straw is fresh, changed daily in the stall,
and the savior has had his own miraculous birth.
Why wait? Pygmy queen, believe in molasses,
oats and corn, in the salvation of your own
vast girth, know that as I kneel here with rags,
someone will be rich, someone caught and saved.

Mud Road

Unmaintained, enter at your own risk.
I risk and run the mutt down, dodging horse plops
and buggy ruts. We trot past the mulberry and
carrion flower. Here, the disdained hang on,
unmowed, unsprayed or cut, and one mile down
in the timber, at least at this hour—
the slight rise, tug in the hamstring,
deep groove in the bark of the bur oak—
even the coons are safe from the Amish boy's
night watch: hound, flashlight, gun.

How I love to reach up and snag a limb,
pull off a mouthful of these berries, purple
staining my hands, my teeth and tongue.
How I love to watch old man Sullivan, the recluse,
ramble through his pasture, green '42 Ford,
visor flopped down against the 7 a.m. sun.
His guernseys part, even though they know
it's futile when this Moses stops to dig a thistle.
Every winter we hear him say: going to sell,
farm's just too big for me now,

but then the spring rains, summer dust,
fall Winesaps and Bartletts weighing down,
the baskets stored on the cellar steps.
And we find ourselves back where we were born,
never leaving, learning to know the candles
in the drawer by touch, the lights out
from the thunderstorm, knowing that we
must get up each morning without fail,

bacon and eggs, the thin puff
of smoke from the chimney, and go out

in this same place to shuttle the cattle
through one rusty gate to another.
I hear Sullivan holler, *git, git, git,*
as the cows cross the path to where the grass
is greener, where the land promises milk,
if not honey, and when a woman and dog jog by,
you can lift your hand and wave back,
knowing that even a half-stranger senses
the real danger of this road, what it feels
to float down a river, banks on each side thick and wild.

Scheherazade

Batteries and blanket, this spring
I've made a little place here
down in the cellar to listen
to the radio crackle the weather:
TORNADO WATCH, high winds and hail,
take cover. In this furnace room,
I'm alone with the centipedes and
cinder blocks, the mouse scurrying
to squeeze in from the rain.
I'm away from all windows and
flying glass, the silver maple
that might crash through the roof.
Overturned bucket, my chair, I see
by an oil lamp on loan from a neighbor.
How dumb to depend on lines from
the world. In these storms, it's no use
to think *phone*, or *pump*, or *switch*.
In the draft, only the dust churns
in the old ducts, their arms
branching up, the octopus.
Outside, the anemones swim along
the grove floor and bend in the inky dark.
Once I knew a man who drove a friend
here from the East, she belted in,
terrified the whole time of a funnel cloud.
Just as they crossed the state line,
the sky clear and cool, he pulled his
VW bug to the side, and ordered her down.
"This is it, quick. The only safe place
underneath." She dove past the

exhaust pipe, crawled and scrunched,
scraping her back, her butt, on the pan.
He stood on the highway and laughed.
Once I lived above a garage, and when
I heard the horns, ran to the owners'
basement, their ninety-year-old mother,
senile, but still strong, nailing shut
the door, crying, "Sindbad, Sindbad,
we're all ruined, lost in the wreck!"
Once I was yanked from sleep, my mother's
hand flying me down the three flights
of steps. That time, the coal room,
and prayers, *Hail, Mary,* while
a twister wound its fury past the house,
ripping up everything in its path.
Our clothesline and poles were found
a mile from town where a barn collapsed
on a man milking cows. *Holy, Mary,*
I answered and pressed my legs together,
trying to stop the pee from wetting
my pants. Upstairs, my father, the engineer,
moved from one window to another,
opening, closing, each a crack, trying
to assure the proper flow of air.
But this year the blows have become
routine—the howl through the attic vents,
feed sacks tumbling across the field
smack into the fence. Two a.m.,
and I'm chewing gum, recounting
other times—the snakebite, car wreck,
doctor goof, the bolt of lightning
so close it fanned the hairs on my arms.
Suddenly, I recall the dryer blowing up,
the bang, the smoke, the flames in the air,

then at age four, the fall from the elm tree,
and at thirty, the drunk who broke in,
and how, from the second story window,
I jumped to safety. Now I sit up
and tell these tales to the mouse.
His black eyes glare back at me.
The two of us know the game.
Where one night ends, another begins
until all is forgiven or simply spent,
forgotten, and the sky relents.

I-80 Lieder

Toyota wagon, seats down,
I'm stretched in the back, feet propped
against the tailgate, speeding the five hour hospital
trip to Chicago. Friends click on the radio, Mahler,
the bass strings humming from both speakers,
and lips pressed, the clouds outside the window
are my dead driven home in old Chevys, in horse-drawn carts.

Buggy and buckboard, the whip snaps
against the mare's flank, and the violins,
the violins echo the tune. Sir Georg Solti lifts the baton.
Milkwagon, meatwagon, down the entrance, up the exit ramp.
Gustav on the Interstate, Gustav on the old cow path, the
     mud road,
conducting the rows of corn, the tumbled down barns and
     towns—
Wilton, Durant, Atalissa: The Vienna Imperial Opera.

Then bring on the viola, the oboe toward Chicago,
Hog Capitol of the World. *Kindertotenlieder*
liederkranz, Toyota Corolla, little garland,
now the station's drifting, fading out. They turn up
the volume as we cross the Mississippi River, the state line,
the cold brown water below, the cellos underscoring the winds,
garland of song, little garland in hand.

Heaven-and-Earth House

Three drops under the tongue—
star-of-Bethlehem, hornbeam, elm—
three 3x/day here at the foot
of Pikes Peak where I've come
in late December for the air,
to eat couscous and kasha,
burdock and kombu: hopes of a cure.

We are the nothing-to-lose ones,
the try-anything-once ones,
weed seeds inside our cells—
dandelion, nettle, lizard tail—
roots sunk in, for it is the tips
that count, reaching out to tap
new moisture. Roots, stems, leaves,
the stomata, those little mouths
opening, closing, sucking in air
in the evening when we boil
wild ginger and sleep in its vapor.
Like cures like, we hear in the morning
when we brush ourselves with
vegetable fiber in the shower,
beat ourselves with our fists.
(This is no crazier than anything else.)

In the next room, a woman has
a tumor growing on her heart—
monk's hood, thistle, lion's foot—
pressing against her windpipe.
For six weeks she has had no voice.

19

If she weeps, she chokes.
So in the night she wraps herself
in a quilt brought from home—
star-of-Bethlehem—and I listen
for her whistles and moans:
carrion flower, black medick.
I tap on the wall and she raps an answer.
I stare out the window at the mountain
I hike higher each day in the snow,
stones slipping under my feet.
I stare out the window into the dark—
star-of-Bethlehem, shooting star, angelica.

More Tests

Here for more tests.
This time the Heidelberg capsule.
Swallow: one tiny radio transmitter
on a string. *Yum.*
I lie on a table while across the room
my scores flash green on the screen—
pH of stomach and colon.
Rum-tum-dittley-dum-tum.

Acid or alkaline, the snow beats
wet drops against the window pane.
The technician leaves me alone,
(the program running fine).
Try to relax, twenty minutes more,
then we'll wait for the print-out.
The snow beats wet drops and
twenty flights below Santa
leans in a doorway, *Dong, din,*
shoppers dropping money in his cup.

Fish on a line, too young
to fry, what treasures do you find
as you nose down, fin through those cold,
dark spots? Oh, beam back tales of
a woman paddling her way to shore
on a raft, beam back casks of
vintage wine, still waiting, unbroken,
uncorked, *rum, dittley-dum,* the long
banquet table set with silver and linen.
Oh, beam back that little beam of light

from the candles, that small coin
of light, shiny, human face on the front
still strong—rough beast on the back
rubbed smooth.

Muskrat

The slow rise—the lap of the wave on the levee,
the mud against the seawall, the water up two feet,
up three, up over the grass, the benches in the park,
up ten feet, over the sidewalks of First Street,
down into the basements, the sewers, down
to the echo of the muskrat in the pipes,
the brick on the toilet to keep it out,
the sandbags in the doorway, the long block
of ice in the middle of the river.

It is under there, gnawing,
breeding, carrying its young by the neck,
there as the planes circle the ice,
dive down over the bank, let go their cargo.
Cinders and ashes fall through the air.
Cinders and ashes fall through the air
like rain, like snow. It is there and the river rises.
The sun shines, the ice cracks, the huge barge-like hulk
moves, melts down by the dam and the river rises.

Then I am under, mouth open, skin puffed,
each pore ballooning, taking the water in.
I swim toward land but hear it above me,
watch the water glide off its back.
Then I am under, floating up, head clearing,
the water spilling from my chin. I shake my hair,
smell its odor and it is there, wrapped around
my shoulders, its fat body a buoy, my arms
dropped around its neck, my face in its fur.

The Art of Acupuncture

Heart, lung, liver, kidney, spleen,
the needle slips in to the wince of pain, then midnight
to midday, the wheel spins round, and underneath, we are all
flesh, all grass, the weed, the blade, the word.

The word is: it hurts at first, then you might feel
a tingling, on opening—*door of the wind, window to the sky.*
And the constellations are scattered across your skin—
water of the milky way, dragon breathing fire.
Up and down your spine, a planisphere of the northern horizon.

Mother and son, fire burns wood, and the needle drives into
        your hand.
Mother and son, wood leaves ash, a cross on your forehead.
And in order to get better, son leaves mother,
a rock rolled up, rolled back.

Rock, air, fire, water, wood.
Each stab is a dare, a bet, a shake of the dice,
so I sing of Pilate and the Roman soldiers,
a spear in the side, a thorn in the crown.
My God, my God, I sing of moxa and mugwort, of lifting cups,

of the Tao and Yellow Emperor, the T'ang and the Ming.
I sing of a heaven of eased muscles, greased joints,
an earth of full moons, the light, the light
to see the way. Some say the world will end in fire,
the cosmos in chaos, but I sing of the curious points,

nameless, of nerve ganglia and meridians,
tiny circles of tissue and skin, holding on,
holding everything in. I shout of these oddballs,
odd ducks, unnoticed halos of hope that neither
crow nor coo, but go on in their wobbly way

grazing in the yard for a bug and, at night,
wings spread, shine in the dark with their faint flicker,
    their dim flame.

Early Frost

Splat of blood, urine stain, long tear
down the center where I caught my toe.
This sheet is shot: PROPERTY OF
HEARTBREAK HOSPITAL, CHICAGO—
ripped off my bed and packed
(I'll tie up my tomatoes)
for the long oxygen tank ride home.
This sheet is hot! the red dot in
the corner directing the laundry cart
to fourth floor, the two heavy
glass doors opening: ISOLATION.
Mask, gown, the puffy halo cap,
red dot in the corner, the month red sun,
day in, night out, over Lake Michigan.

This sheet is hot on the first cold
night in September, the blue earth
spinning further away from the sun.
This sheet is not intact,
strips torn, binding vines to poles.
Touch when dry: these plants will snap.
Touch when wet: fungus will spread
through the leaves and leave holes.
I drape what's left, this holey sheet,
over lettuce, chard, beet greens—
their hard red suns shriveling beneath ground—
and pray for one day more, I'll eat.

Father Di Pilato
at Veteran's Auditorium

Blindness, be gone!
And there he shouts into a microphone as the healed
spill onto the stage, cataracts dissolving,
trickling down their faces like tears.

Deafness, be gone!
And there he claps his hands three times behind an old nun
who falls to the floor, the spirit slain.
A Vietnam vet sticks his fingers in his ears
and the mine forever under his foot sinks
back into the ground, intact.

Satan, come out!
And here I close my eyes, praying, really praying
for the first time in years, swaying back and forth
to the organ in a crowd of three thousand.

Back pain, neck pain, leg and foot pain,
paralysis, lumbago and limp, come out!
Put down your crutches, braces, canes.
Walk to me. Now!

And now a young girl in the bleachers screams,
her one short leg growing three inches longer.
Her platform shoe tossed into the air,
she runs down across the foul line.

Cancers, tumors, heart disease,
lung disease, gum disease,
in the name of Jesus Christ, come out!

And now I am linking arms, singing, right here
in section F, eyes rolled up to the basketball hoops.
Lord, God, let this illness, all those old sorrows inside me, out.
Oh, Sweet Jesus, out, out, out!

II

Dutchman's Breeches

Van Dry, Van Wilt, Van Sickle—
O, ye of little faith, another winter without snow,
    another April creek gone.
But clothespin to seam, six blossoms to a stem,
    the Dutchman's breeches hang on the line.

And here are the bloodroot, the toothwort,
    Mayapple and trillium, the small under my heel—
six strong men when I need them:
    Van Patter, Vandewater, Vanglen.

    O, ye of little hope, when the trees rain,
unrolling their canopy, the ash leaves
    crumble, and the earth, able to absorb more,
steps closer.

    O, ye of little heart, hoof, wing—
crop for crop, the pelicans return,
    skimming the slough, while the wild hogs
rout under the fence with their young
    for last year's corn, and the owl retrieves
the shrew impaled on the locust thorn.

Novena

Eye of potato, thin neck of cabbage
arching out of the ground, I kneel
here in late April

and sprinkle ash on roots and stems.

Ash of oak, ash of pine, ash of elm
sifting into the dirt, paper ash,

ash to keep moths from drilling through the leaves,
ash to keep stalks from curling up, slinking away.

Ash of ash
blown down in a storm, logs sawed and split,

logs I carry in my arms,
while the warm ash waits through the winter,
sinking to the bottom of the stove.

Ash like snow, like skin.

Cool ash loose in the house at night,
settling in my lungs
as I sleep,

as I walk out into the dark,
a bucket of ash in my hand.

And in the morning,
my face on the pillow in ash.

Ode to Okra

Mumbo, jumbo, pot-full-of-gumbo, o sweet okra,
red stem, pink blossom, only plant in the garden
to survive this summer's heat, wilt, grasshopper drought.

And there is no cure for this plague:
guinea hens, traps, sprays, hand-picking won't stop
these insects from stripping leaves,
chewing through the screen door.

Rain fifteen inches down, their eggs never drowning,
these bugs just keep on fucking—two, three, four
generations at once hovering on the fence,
waiting to begin their chomping.

And there is no help for the poor
tomatoes, potatoes, lettuce, turnips, squash.
They've all collapsed into mush.

All but my beautiful, ugly okra.
Seed pods: sliced, diced, rolled in corn meal,
fried in a pan. Cut up and dropped into soups,
stew pots in the winter to stretch further.

Take me in, sweet meat, teach me the secret
of your stalks, eye high by the Fourth of July.
Heal me with the nod of your leaves,

the deep veins and lobes, bundles of fibers,
the thin layer of skin covering your bud scars,
the shimmer of each new flower.

Jackpot

We're all here in Vegas—the look-alike Elvis,
Ringo Starr, Sammy Davis Jr. . . .
I shuffle into the clinic with the other
arthritic for one more quack cure, drop
my money in the slot. Oh, it's hot!
The handle too warm to touch, the desert sun
outside bleaching the lizard's skull.
I bet on the reptiles, on the scaly-skinned,
the spadefoot toad who burrows backward
and sleeps seven feet down in the sand.
I go with the insects who breed and feed at night,
with the single-celled protozoan protected
from the heat by its own cyst.
I bet on the woman on the couch with
a growth on her cheek, the seven-year-old
in cowboy boots with eczema head to toe.
I roll for the shaky hand, spastic muscle, drooling lip.
I roll for the palsied girl that she may walk,
the diapered man that he may no longer drip.
For I have faith in the communion of waiting rooms
and know the inside secret of wheelchairs,
IV poles, crutches and canes.
I know the woman weeping on the examining table.
She raises the ante and bets on Death Valley.
I bet on the shuttle bus back to the motel near the casino,
the ice machine, the clean plop into the bucket,
the fresh towels and Gideon Bible in the desk drawer.
I bet on the Book of Mormon next to the fish tank,
the Newsweek with Oliver North on the cover.
Yes, I roll for the silver dollar, the neon,

34

salamander and tadpole, the quickie marriage of the
kissing gouramis behind the glass. I wait for the
cloudburst, the once-or-twice-a-year puddle,
the underground tests to explode.

Frog Gig

It took a whole plateful to make a meal—
food #7 I could eat without blacking out—
those little white pairs of pantaloons.

Oh, I'd pithed Kermits—needle from the tray,
lab partner, scholarshipped wrestler, locking
thumb and index finger around the squirmer's neck.

No, it was the pileup of those limbs, steamed and soggy
like wet laundry, that made me pick the tendons
from my teeth with special care, and know

those doctors lied who said it'd taste like chicken.
These were no white feathers beside a red wheelbarrow
glazed with rain, no Sunday dinners, the whole family

gathered in the kitchen, home from ten o'clock Mass,
still singing hymns, pressure cooker on the stove
so my grandmother could gum her portion.

Once, due to expense, I went out with friends
to Corker's Pond, the water quiet, clear.
Tiny piece of bandanna dangling from the end

of a fishing line, we groped through the dark,
sun going down, and followed their croaks and plops,
our hooks tangling in the cattails. We lay on the bank

for hours and held our rods just above their heads,
but not one hopped at the cloth, not one crooned
so much depends upon, nor shot out its forked tongue.

Coyote-Fox

My neighbor claims a coyote-fox,
this thing that slinks up from the creek
at night and takes our ducks.
Long-legged and red, he says he's seen
it in the yard as late as eight,
jaws clamped tight on wings.

Weasel or mink, it's not, teeth marks
in the wrong spot, too big for coon,
and Rudy's first shot nabbed the stray
yellow cat. No, this is some cross,
this shaggy trickster-beast.
Down by the river where Dirty Face

feeds in, it howls at the full moon,
then waits till dawn to sneak up
on the sheep and gnaw a leg, a thigh,
the poor ewe too stunned to bleat.
My neighbor says its tail is dog—
little clumps of mud hang from its fringe.

Its eyes are something else.
They glow, dart about and know the ins
and outs of holes too small for loyalty
to squeeze in. At midnight I've tried
to catch a glimpse of the local sphinx,
but when I think I've spied a pointed ear,

it's a leaf on the gooseberry shrub.
When I think I've heard the click of paws
on gravel, the road unwinds its empty riddle.
My neighbor set a trap and hoped
to cage it whole, load it in his truck
and drive it live five miles to Shiloh.

No bait works. Not chicken heads nor fish.
The doors trip, slam shut but morning chores
find the Havahart too much of a sop
and us ready to try again with leaner cuts.
It's easy. We could scan the ridge and
understand full well who owns this land.

We could grasp the risk. Instead,
we hold on tight to what we think
we have, and fear this hunk of ditch fur.
At dusk, we gather up the fowl, lock,
and sleep right here inside the coop.
For weeks, a sweat-stained shirt hung

a top a beam, the smell of humans
sure to scare away the beast. But then,
at last, when it swiped through the second
batch of chicks, we vowed to guard the perch.
Mallard, Khahki, Muscovy, at two,
still up, wake on this barn bench,

I peer inside my ribs and offer my heart
as meat. I offer my lungs, these sacks
of grain gleaned from the fields
when the machines have had their fill.
I try to make a truce, a peace.
I try to wish us back before the corn

when the grass bent this way and that
with the wind. At four, the cross inches close—
a sniff, a look, the clank of metal—
but no one's fooled. The whole lure
disappears, is carried off in the dark
to some nettle-hidden den teeming with young.

Stay Still, Duck

Do not think of yourself huddled in the corner
of the coop, the mad rooster charging
my shin, pecking, *tat-a-tat-tat*.
Do not think of my hands grabbing your neck,
stretching it over the block, your eyes open,
beak shut, crop stuffed with the corn I bought
from the shy Amishman. Fold your wings in,
forget South, the cold north winds blowing down,
the cold steel blade, and oh, God, the blade again,
your quills pulled out one by one, pitched
in a sack on the ground. Do not think of your body
swinging over the flame, down singeing,
loosening pin feathers that will not give.
Give up, duck, give in, forget your flesh
slit sternum to anus, gizzard bigger than
my fist, liver shimmering fish-like
in the October night, my fingers swimming up,
steady now, surrounding the tiny gallbladder
so it will not break and taint your delicate dark meat.
Forget your heart anchored to your ribs,
tendons taut to my yank and tug.
Forget your heart, stuck this way
inside your house for a year.
Your number's up, duck, forget.
Forgive.

Take Two

Together, cameras in hand,
we witnessed the birth of the goat,
head and hoof slipping out,
the short squawks of the mother,
her eyes fixing ours,
the first real time she'd let us near.

"Sell her," you'd said,
as day after day in the pasture,
she turned and ran when you
inched close, offering your hand.

But there, splayed in the straw,
she held us, pupils a steady line
from *capra* to human,
you coaching her on.
Good girl, that's fine.
Then the shoulders, the rib cage
striped in white, the little buck
fully encased in its bag—
and the nanny, with a kick,
a quick bite, cleaning him off,
standing him up on his feet to suck.

We stood there, too, not really
knowing what more to do,
afraid to stroke our doe.
So we shot film and listened
to her cries again. The afterbirth
passed and she ate it down.
You rocked the kid in your lap.

That night you paced the room
and would not calm,
would not let me near.
No hand nor heart would help.
The world, the world was
water bursting and we were all
tumbling out into a filthy stall,
stillborn.

They say a goat
will soothe a horse,
the one a balm for the other.
We tried our nanny on the filly,
and the horse stopped her wild bolting,
came trotting up the road at a perfect pace.

But would our doe tame?
Then, when we approached the fence,
she hid between the mare's flanks.
If we reached out for a pat,
we risked a strike.

The buck, stroked and held
from the first, three-pound ball
of fur tucked in an elbow,
romped across your back,
pawed your leg for treats.
That's the secret.
When you're grown, you're gone.

When you were young,
were hands hooves
that kicked and bucked?
Did heads butt, the horns

clacking, the hollow sound
carrying all across the valley?

Once, we penned the doe against
the woodpile, and you threw
your arms around her neck.
"I'll hug her till she tames."
For an hour, we fed her oatmeal
and beans from our fingers,
smoothed her fur. Yet
the slightest loosening
of our grip sent her dashing
back to the barn.

Please understand,
I mean no harm.
If I could roll back film,
I'd be there from the first,
a close-up shot.
Frame after frame would
jump-cut, zoom to my arms,
hands that would not drop.
Then the dark force
at the fence might blur,
the grass take on a different sheen.
Then the tree might sweep down,
its limbs bending, lush and green.
Then the world, the world
might be water washing
down over the leaves,
clearing the day's must,
and neither the bough, the bough,
nor you would break.

No Wonder

No wonder we missed the lagoon that day in
late July, your last in town. We turned down
the T-road, south, then back again, north,
the gravel pinging against the bumper of the truck,

dust swelling up, the road fogging. We tried to retrace
the route we'd wound a year before and became lost,
but after a summer of driving, we no longer cared,
loving each white farm house, the large Amish

gardens bordered with cannas. And those flowers would have
been enough. We could've driven home happy, the petals
folded down into the creases of both our memories.
But then, we tried to find the curve beyond a stand of elms,

that sinkhole that had opened: five great blue herons,
necks pulled in, wading among the cattails and Indian grass.
Necks stretched out, dagger-like bills shot down
into the water, and up with minnows. Or air.

We knew we had to be on the wrong road, that a place
just couldn't disappear. You remembered the Sunday
school house on the left and the one-lane bridge over the creek.
I knew we hadn't gone beyond 22, so all afternoon

we kept on, the herons' wings fading into the slate sky.
Round and round, for the third time, we passed the same
buggy full of teen-age girls, bare feet sticking out.
We kept on, this one last puzzle between us, impossible

to solve, never thinking of the weather, the sun glaring,
the thunderstorm clouds that gathered, then left us three
    months
without rain, subsoil moisture fifteen inches down.
Dust on our tongues, we drove home, cracks swallowing
    the ground.

Two Skulls

We hope to sketch their bones, but do not want their meat,
the stench floating through our house for days.
So, tonight we open the cold October dirt
and the moon shines down through the scarecrow's eyes.

The moon shines down through the scarecrow's eyes
and the cow skulls lower into the garden holes.
Dug up in spring, flesh stripped worm-clean in the April haze,
the bones, cast in clay, become our vessels.

And the cow skulls lower into the garden holes,
their eyes staring through us, still in place, tongues bitten
      in two.
The bones, cast in clay, become our vessels,
our study of form, texture, color, tone.

Their eyes staring through us, still in place, tongues bitten
      in two—
in silence we lean against our spades—
our study of form, texture, color, tone—
then draw the dirt back over their eyes like shades.

The Cat and the Fiddle

Hey, diddle, diddle, the cow
jumped down, the whole kit and
caboodle, and you the moon.
Driving north from town, Galway City,
Whit Sunday, Auntie May at the wheel,
you didn't know what to feel,
the windshield black and cracked,
the little tuft of fur caught
in the wiper. *Poor dumb beast*,
Auntie May slammed on the brakes.
The bovine slid from bonnet to ditch,
switched her tail into the air
to signal the end of danger.

Your whole life seat-belted and strapped,
you never set out without the tire check,
map, extra blanket, jack and flares.
You never pulled all-nighters,
but thumb grasped to pinkie, be prepared,
read ahead to a fault, Descartes
breaking apart before the sun
came out to shine on Plato's cave.
And here, you knew a moment before
she flew, the Tom rosining his bow,
the dish and spoon calling ahead
for reservations. But if there's
anything to say, it's this:

sometimes the cat may break
a string, or the dog sink into

a deep depression, but not to relax
and shout for Guinness all around.
At most, pull over and share candy
from May's pocketbook, brown and worn,
tell jokes of the Kerryman measuring
the miles to Dublin by the number of
pedestrians knocked down. For up a bit,
is another bucolic scene, on either side
of a winding road cut between two cliffs,
a herd of Holsteins grazes on the green
grass, bobbing their heads toward the sea.

On the Orval Yoder Turnpike

Were we lucky. This time a steer calf
in the beams and the moon too low to see—
only a shadow across the windshield,
then the radiator spurting steam,
the grill and headlight splintering
on the blacktop, and the soft moan
of an animal not harmed enough.
It could've been twenty below, the wind

drifting snow against the fence, the hole
wide enough to let the entire herd through.
We could've been bruised and cut,
the children pitched head-first into
the night, their *grossmami* right behind.
We could've been charged by the bull
in the ditch—black angus—a blur before us.
What matters: we're all safe, no one hurt,

the farmer at home and easily found.
That's the main thing. And from years
of practice, the slit across the throat
was firm and swift, the calf bled out
before the sheriff even picked up the call.
Block and tackle, the butchering was done
by ten, the children fed soup and tucked in bed.
It could've been a real mess, so much worse.

Gulf

In this town, 1941, they burned
Chester Yoder's effigy in the square.
Stuffed with straw, it went up faster
than ditch grass on a drought day.
After so many months without rain,
all it takes is a spark,
then the fields are aflame.

After so many years without bombs,
we remember Chester again, the first
Amish here to face the draft,
Old Order, German speaker,
the man so many called traitor,
the one who clung to his belief
that no matter who or how,
killing was wrong. Even after
his job as a forest fighter,
some turned and crossed the street,
others called him "yellow" and spat.

Now we wrap the trees with ribbons
to welcome home heroes who flew
over the cradle, and when the tree
rocked and the wind blew, flames
spread for miles in all directions.
Let's give them a hand. Or an arm.
Or the moustache Chester still shaves
off every morning in protest against
the old commanders in the country
his ancestors fled for freedom.

Let's let them atone for all the shame
we felt in the past, battles unwon,
hay never put up in the barn.
To bear, each year the hard ground
needs blessing, so let's sprinkle
our seeds with water, blood and oil.
Let's sit down with Chester at the table
and lower our heads in prayer, for now
when the bread breaks, so does the bough
and even Chester can never fight that fire.

Shunning

The doors are always closed to those we know
too well. The well brings up our deepest sin.
To those who stray so far, we must say no.

Amish store: suspenders, hook and eye.
We cannot sell our wares to half our kin,
for the doors are always closed to those we know.

We cannot wave or stop and say hello
to ones who go beyond the daily norm.
To those who stray so far, we must say no.

To some we may seem hard, or mean, or more,
to lock our families out in such a storm,
but we hang on to ours in rain or snow.

Without rules, where would we be now?
Lost souls, by the masses taken in,
like men who hold the sword and not the plow.

A knock. Oh, no, we mustn't even go.
The pain of holding out, is holding in.
The doors are always closed to those we know,
and we leave nothing, no one in the cold.

The Day

The day you have to stay on the other side
of the fence, teat and milk still in sight,
brimful, hanging from the belly of your nanny.
How lovely her blue fur, brown eyes,
ears, stiff and white, flicking away flies.
How perfect the curl of her tail, the sharp
tips of her horns, the split of her hooves.
How you can still feel your head butting
her bag to start the flow, then how
everything moves, tongue pressed against skin,
mouth tilting up and up again. The day began
the same with sun and corn, the rooster's crow,
a quick leap from the woodpile, but one look
into that water pail was enough, your own
face blurring. This is it, kid, you're grown,
teeth too big for baby stuff. So quit your
moans and peek through the slats
at the wild grape just a neck stretch within reach.
What you don't know, what you don't know.

Cooped

The cluck, the quack, the coo,
Chanticleer's gusty *er-er-er-er-ooo*.
After a night content in boxes
or balanced on rough beams, safe
and locked away from the fox,
they long for the dawn, for the heavy
door to swing open, the plank let down.

Bantam and Cochin, they listen for
the moment I fiddle with the latch
(what a fudge) and the first thin
stream of light slips in. Leghorn
and Sultan, Blue Andalusians,
this is half the fun, to see which turkey
leaves her nest first, heads the line,

eggs snatched up while she breakfasts.
A scratch in the dirt, the hen and tom,
straw kicking up, a bug, a beak
in the pond, the puddle in the yard,
then it's back to business, hatchlings
learning their lessons at the speckled
wings of their moms, each day's venture

a little farther, each peck a direct strike.
But, oh, to be shut in, to be forced
to depend on something so human.
Crèvecoeur, crèvecoeur, weep and wail,
gobble and shriek for all the broken shells
and hearts. We must wait, wait, and remember
that this is just another night, the moon

up again. I imagine it may be this way
at the end: all huddled together, cramped,
the other's claw poking your lung,
the thirst so strong it claims your name.
Then the squeak of the hinge, and good layers
and bad, fine feathers and clipped wings,
strut, scurry and flap at once into the sun.

III

The Orderly

Tubes, dressings, pitchers, cups.
    These are the things I fix up.
Soon you'll catch on to the routine.
    Every morning into the bath,
I.V. pole rolled to the water's edge
    then I tie on a fresh gown.

The sheets on this cart shouldn't be
    folded like that. And whoever left
those blankets a mess? Oh, I'll keep track
    of temperature, pressure,
color, weight. All charted by ten.
    I'll put down what you eat, drink,

what finally comes out. I'll wheel you
    away to x-ray your lungs, and up
to the O.R. for this scope or that.
    We will become friends. I'll meet
your relatives, learn to recognize
    your husband's voice on the phone.

"She's in the testing room now and
    can't talk." I'll keep you walking
up and down the halls to maintain
    muscle tone and—that's right,
(I'm an expert at changing a bed
    with the patient in it.)—

roll toward the rail a minute.
    And when you return . . .

Oh, you all come back. I won't be able
    to recall your name, nor you mine.
It's the funniest thing. I'll remember
    you, if I do, as the hole in the heart,

or the one whose virus crossed the
    blood-brain barrier. And you'll
know me as the carrier of linens and
    lunch trays, the orderly who kept
the unit orderly, the balding man
    who'd been a medic in Nam

and knew what it was to wake at two,
    sweating for no reason.
(I'll leave your tongue depressors
    here on your table by your bed for
the doctor.) You'll recall our conversations
    about not knowing what's happening

in the night, how snipers were little
    guys who fired out of nowhere,
ours, farm boys, good with a rifle,
    loners, who could suck in their breath
and grieve silently when they thought
    they hit one of their own.

Home, you'll remember how hard it was
    here, then long to be back where
at least someone would answer your light,
    that orderly who knew how to stop
the rolling of the T.V. screen, keep
    a watch on the blood drip, give

a good enema, deal a game of hearts,
    that orderly who could be quiet and
listen, the one who knew that all human
    misery came down to this:
eye on the sight, the brush of a hand,
    the slow squeeze of a finger.

Dear Diary,

You should see me here all dressed in white—
surrounded by your blank pages. The doctors are
trying to find out why my sight has grown so dim.

I'm still too young for a cane. So, it's dilate
and test, read this chart with left and right.
They measure so little—just one pair of wings

unfolding in my field for miles. You know,
that even with the fog hovering over the hills
in the morning, my pasture goes on forever.

Some say it's all scientific, that once you record
the facts: wind shift, temperature dip, you can
predict their coming, those monarchs streaming south,

each year a new generation, landing time
and again on the same trees along their route
toward night to roost before the moon comes up again.

Labor Day weekend. That's usually the week for
their rest stop, yet who but me can fathom how,
after thousands of miles in the air, they know

where to go? Some say they navigate by the sun,
some say the stars. But no one's ever explained
why they come back to that precise elm near the pond.

And who but me can sense the exact moment
their legs cling to branches, their bodies mimicking
bark, needles, leaves? Some say it's all coincidence.

Maybe. More likely the eye spots on their wings
are mine, blind, but as true as any predator's.
It's such a game, the way we all strive to look

the same and learn to leave each other alone.
Monarchs eat milkweed, that toxic weed that kills
birds on first bite, then the viceroy falls in line,

spreading its Halloween wings, the perfect
costume. And what of our masks? The treats
that rattle at the bottom of our bags?

This I will say, the trick is up tonight somewhere
on this ward. Scales rubbed thin, someone will
light for the last time, fold in, a house of cards.

The nurses gave us these books to record our scores:
fever, racing pulse, drop in weight from the start.
We write down what we ate, if we react to paint

or soap, if our lids swell, flutter or blink
with a change of clothes or air. I notice these
things, and more. My body has no secrets,

but I've told only you, paper. I scrawl on you
these letters and wish you'd take this gift from me
and burn it up, set it on flame, orange and black

fire and smoke drifting into the sky. Below,
a horse grazes the ground and doesn't even glance up
when thousands of tiny spirits beat furiously by.

Kathleen

Hey, Tex, want to dance?
Yeah, you in the cowboy boots.
I know, nights mostly, you wheel
those litters to the freight elevator,
your white gown on backwards, the ties
flapping open in front over the snaps
of your western shirt. *Do-sa-do*
then down you go, and grand right left
onto the slab. Let me see,
once I'm in the cooler,
who will sign the papers?
The sobbing mother fresh from
her bridge club, or the all-
in-your-head-remarried-in-
a-month husband who will bend
to your wish for the advancement
of science? *Gents, honor your partner,*
honor your corner, and take 'er on home.
So bring in the forms. Oh, I've seen
you in the halls long before it's time.
Tex, the outrider, just wants things
in order. But me, you don't suspect,
and let those spurs ride right by.
Instead, you hover over the ones
who've rung the dishrag and circled
round them all. *Promenade eight*
'til you get straight, now ready
for the call. And you be steady
when you cut in and try to determine
the mysteries of my brain. Will you

find the gaps, the breaks, the lapse
in synapses accounting for my fall?
Will you find the grit and gravel
loping along the trails of those
tiny blood vessels? Or will I come out
clean? No one able to quite say
what went wrong. *Sashay left and fly away.*
Stay, Tex, and whistle me the tune
you do every morning at seven,
green scrubs, instruments sterilized
clean on the tray, fluorescent lights
flicked on and swinging from the
basement beams, toothpick in the corner
of your mouth as you set out
across the Rancho Grande. Oh, play
me the chisel, the scalpel, the saw.
I'm ready to meet my pistol
packin' mama, my turkey in the straw.

Rosary Manto, L.P.N.

This time, a forty-year-old female. I wheel her into the
storeroom.

Close eyes. Close mouth.

They mostly go at night—my shift. Why work it? Pays more.
Since coming to the States, I take what nobody else wants,
and get my share. Eleven to seven. It's quieter, yes, some.
But don't assume it means sleep, a game of hearts with the
orderlies at the desk. At twelve we make rounds. Up and
down the ward with a flashlight, poke my head in the door,
listen for the breathing. I shine on the bed for the count.
Census goes in at one in the morning.

Insert dentures
if possible. If dentures will not stay in, place in cup and tape
to the chest.

Good, this one has teeth of her own.
And a husband and daughter at home. The doctor will make
that call. But he won't be able to tell them anything more
than me. Midnight, she was fine. At four when I went in
again, gone.

Pad and tie ankles
together. Bend elbows, pad and tie wrists together. Tape
wedding ring to finger.

Oh, they always go when no one's looking,
although she made sure of it. Sometime between checks,

she split those bed sheets into strips and looped them over
the grate in the bathroom ceiling. Then up on the toilet seat,
and boom. I'd read her chart, knew her pain. And who's to
say she was wrong?

DO NOT

remove tubes, drains, casts.

                Soon after I was born, my mother
took a razor to her wrist the same place the soldiers bound
her during the burning of Manila. When the bombing began
and the Yanks moved in, the Japs who were trapped in the
city, went crazy. Buildings burst into flames all around.
Soldiers stabbed babies with bayonets and dragged young
women through smoke and haze into crumbling rooms. My
mother's screams rose with the wail of the sirens.

*Pack rectum with cotton balls, pack vagina or tie off penis
and diaper.*

                The Yanks did "return." This time
with tanks not polo ponies. And my mother waited until
I was weaned. Then I lived in a home and the nuns taught
me to read and write, say my prayers, to stay out of the way
of the twiner at the river where I used to love to go and watch
him twist the fibers, splice ends together and reel them in like
the strings of a kite.

                *Change or reinforce
dressings as necessary. Stamp 2 ID tapes with the patient's
addressograph. The first is placed on the patient's left upper
arm. The second is taped in place on the bottom of the
opposite foot.*

ROSARY MANTO, L. P. N.

The nuns taught me to add and subtract,
to know I couldn't grab from another child's plate, or pull
the tail from the gecko scampering up the wall. We slept five
to a bed and were forbidden bad dreams.

Remove mattress from cart.
Pin the sheet around the body. Place the large morgue sheet
on the cart diagonally. Place the body on the cart.

Now I work nights,
wake sometimes in the light, and stare at the ceiling, not
knowing who or where I am, then slowly I see my name,
floating above water, tough and strong. I remember

Pin the sheet around the body. Pin loosely over face.

I buy milk, rice, bananas, every Wednesday at the corner
grocery. Two mangoes—All Saints' Day, on sale, over-ripe,
and pretend they're for my mother's grave, her favorite food.
But I don't even know where her spirit lands. Maybe she
never touches down. In the end, I bring the fruit home on
the bus to a room where I live six blocks from this hospital.
I must be careful when I walk to work alone in the dark.
On break I eat mangoes myself, and remember at twenty
I came to this country for more opportunity. And I've
had plenty.

The Doctor Explains

In all my forty years of practice,
I've only had two similar cases.
And let's get clear from the start:
I deal with difficult patients
presenting a myriad of symptoms—I don't
have to tell you—ranging from minor
skin irritations to cardiac arrest.
Of course, those of you hospitalized
here are without doubt the most
severe, given little hope of recovery
until you made the discovery
on your own that my research has proven
effective and I am one of a handful
of doctors in the country who can help.
Toxic poisoning. I am the world's
foremost authority, the first man
called in on the scene in the early
hours of the Bhopal accident.
I went over with a team of physicians
specially picked by the president.
But back to the present and our event
last night. As I said, I've had only
two other similar experiences.
One was a man from Arizona who owned mines,
worked his way up, a true Horatio Alger,
dirt poor kid, picked copper and lead
from the canyons until his hands bled,
then put himself through school at night.
The man became photophobic among other things,
he lived so much in the dark, and later,

perhaps unrelated, his retina detached.
Blind, he ran his whole business by phone.
He'd come for appointments and wrap up
a million dollar deal in the waiting room
on the cellular he carried in his briefcase.
When he wheeled back to my office,
(after his eyes came crippling joint pain)
he always had an investment he wanted
to sell me and was rather funny in his
single-minded determination to make his
business his life. He wouldn't bend
for a soul and kept on urging me to jump
in when the market was hot. I found seven
different kinds of metal filings in his bloodstream
and a residue of dangerous gases in his lungs.
He had begun my detoxification program
and was making slow progress until
several of his veins began to dry up
and his sons fought each other silly
over which one was to become heir apparent
once the father went. The night he did,
he called me from South Africa in terrible pain,
and was throwing all the blame on himself
for his failures. This was new for a guy
who all along had suspected others—
his brother-in-law, his workers,
even his lawyers of plotting his ruin.
But there was nothing I could do from
so far away to adjust his medication.
The second patient, oddly enough, was the man's
daughter whom I first glimpsed when she pushed
his chair into my clinic. "My seeing eye dog,"
he joked and gestured toward her.
She was willowy, thin, but had the same

determined lines around the chin, the same
patch of baldness over the parietal bone,
unusual for a woman. But I sensed
a strong genetic link in all clinical
aspects that had perhaps been exaggerated
by the mother's early death. Or again,
the daughter's thyroid gland may have
become suppressed by radiation she picked up
in the desert where she lived alone with
her father and kept his books. Right next
to a nuclear testing site. At any rate,
she called me at home (I can still
remember, interrupting dinner. We were
just about to sit down to a plate of
pesto. I have a mind to never again
answer the phone.) and complained of
weight loss, that anything she put
in her mouth made her sick—many of you
have experienced a like condition—
and would I see her that very evening.
Of course, she'd also developed
a sensitivity to all chemicals in the air:
perfume, smoke, new carpet smell,
that sort of exposure most of you know,
a function of a damaged immune system.
I told her to come in first thing
in the morning and she agreed that
would be fine, but then at ten,
she called back, more upset, and we
made arrangements for her to be hospitalized
the next day early as possible. At noon,
I ran my finger down the list of new admits
and found her name instead on the print-out
from the morgue. I have no idea what happened

between our last conversation and the time
the maid found her in the motel
up the street. Which brings us down
to Kathleen and the incident in 551.
A code was called by the nurses
at four a.m. and this was the first
I heard anything was out of the ordinary.
Oh, we were all aware Kathleen was
down, but you couldn't be here
and not have faced a lot. Just yesterday
afternoon, the psychologist wrote a report
stating that things were not yet desperate,
so I didn't put the nurses on alert.
No, there are moments out of our control.
And I suppose this will always be
a mystery. I have informed her husband
in California and he will fly in tonight.
That's all I have to say.
Since there are no questions, you may
all go back to your rooms, record your
own temperatures on your charts and
the staff and I will continue our rounds.

Prime Cut

Praise the Lord and pass the setting gel.
Honey, I thought I knew what hell was until I entered
this hospital. First time, flown in on a stretcher
from our little town in central Nebraska. One of our
elders, you know, a rich rancher, loaded me in the back
of his little plane, catheter in my heart, and we
buzzed up over those feedlots, then down again on
a concrete runway. Put a scare into my whole family, Melvin
at home trying to keep the garage going and take care
of the boys. They's there on the bedside table. All four.
Crank that stand up and get a better look at their picture
while you reach me them bobby pins. The sins of the father?
Well, if that verse's true, my daddy must've done something
real bad for me to end up here. And it's just too sad
to think my twins might some day pay for my mistakes.
Sakes alive, just look at their little faces. That's them,
the younger ones in jeans and the cowboy hats. You can tell
them apart from their belt buckles. Look real close
and read the letters: Bret and Chett. The older two
is nearly grown now and I don't worry so much about them,
you know, stars on the football team. 'Course, in Wolbach,
there're so few, every boy who can walk makes first string.

My trouble? Legs just go out from under me, paralyzed.
All of a sudden like, I'm on my knees and can't move.
Doctor made me close down my shop with all the sprays
and permanent waves. The air was so bad in there, not
something anybody might realize. But my, I used to have
the basement of my house fixed up real cute with two
styling booths, the pump-up chairs covered with hides,

Angus and Hereford. And when I draped that cape around
a customer's neck, you could just settle in and relax.
Honey, it ministered to me to dig my fingers down and
massage a scalp, my knuckles swaying in the saddle.
Get along little doggies! Riding up the Chisholm Trail.

Now, if I could've just done her hair. You know,
the one down the hall who, dear Lord, I can hardly say it . . .
She'd been on this ward in isolation for nine months,
near the nurse's station the first time I come, but we
didn't chat much, I was so far out of it, but I knowed
she had a daughter and showed her the twins' school photos
from my billfold. And this week while I'm here again
for more tests, I seen her in the single room when
we pulled the chairs out into the hall for the prayer meeting.
Oh, she looked thin. I stuck my head in the door and
asked her to join, but she said she had her own religion.
And even then, I had a flash of going home back to work,
just itching to have her bend her head back over
my shampoo bowl, suds foaming, the water shooting
out of the rinse hose. I'll tell you, ah, sorry, did I
get that curler too tight? It does a woman right
to trim off the bangs, the fuzzy split ends, comb out
a do like nobody else in town. Separates a person from
the herd, and my word, the thrill when you spin around
in the chair and see yourself for the first time in the mirror!

Just a Dumb Farmer

I'm just a dumb farmer
who didn't know no better.
Listen, son, I don't know how come
you worked your way to this ward,
but if you still think of farming as
be-your-own-boss, outdoors, clean air,
you've got another thing coming.
My whole life, hogs, slop and mud
is what I trudged through.
Finished high school, then
married a good wife and together
we worked hard for what we got—
four kids and seven hundred acres
of soil: beans and corn.
We drained the potholes and plowed
fencerow to fencerow. Even took
the trees down by the river
and cultivated right up to the bank.
Stopped the four crop rotation way back
and did what the government said.
Prices up for higher production.
Sold off most of the livestock.
The reason? See, half the place
used to be pasture, but by nature,
a guy goes with what pays. We let
the manure spreader rust, the hay
rot in the loft, and bought spray.
After the war, all the fellas made
the same change, wanted to be modern.
You'd drive into town to the cafe

and there they'd all be, inside
on a rainy day, debating the price
of fertilizer and pesticide, how
one brand had increased yields
ten times over, and another was
best suited to the new hybrid seed.
We didn't need to worry so much
about cockleburs and buttonweed.
That stuff killed everything off.
And we put our time into pricing
larger combines. Expand, bigger is
better was the word until just
a few years ago when the whole deal
went flat. Yup, I read the label
where they say to wear mask and gloves
but I wouldn't be caught dead.
They're too damn hot. You just
can't. And then I used to spout
the same thing as everyone:
this stuff is so safe a person
could drink it, pour it over
your breakfast cereal. I really
didn't think there was anything
to worry about. Why, we was doing
all right, even planning on going
somewheres warm that winter,
but as soon as I'd get the morning
chores done, it'd start in—the coughing.
I never made no connection, and hell,
it's taken a year of chasing
from that doctor to this to get here.
Rickety-rat-tat-boom. I'm
wheezing every twenty minutes
like an old threshing machine.

At night I count them puffs of steam
instead of sheep. Yup, I'm awake.
Well, meet me in the lounge and
we'll have a game of cards.
Tat-rat-rickety-boom. Around this place
I never miss a trick. To be sure,
I hear every click of a chart,
the squeak of the nurse's feet.
I've learned the calls, code red
for fire, blue for the auctioneer's cane
swatting you on the behind for
the final time. Oh, they drive you down,
all slamming together in the flock at first,
then they sort you out, one by one,
dance down the chute and through the gate.
At any rate, wait for the change
of shift, (they have to do a body count),
then bring your deck and shuffle 'em up good.
We'll wait out the night together,
and I don't know much, but I'll bet on
this for sure: with a little luck,
this old ram will turn the sun up once't more.

Peelings

Sister, pull the curtain.
No, not for the bedpan,
but to scoot your chair closer.
You've been so good, here every day,
I hesitate to ask more, but tonight the question
plays over and over: how much longer?
Oh, wouldn't it be nice to be in our little house
in Vence where we open the windows out to the meadow
filled with poppies and tangerine trees? Orange.
I lie hour after hour, staring at the lightbulb
in that lamp over the bed, then everything seems rimmed
in peelings—the intercom, the nurse's caps, the strings
that tie this gown around my neck. I'm encased in
this room and if I could pull away the rind of this illness,
it's been so long, I wonder what might be left underneath.
My skin. No one can understand the pain of being touched.
Or not. The problem: not even a rash to show the staff
bustling in at 6 a.m. Disappointing, I'm sure, for the interns.
And difficult for any visitor to believe that I'm not
just grieving for some lost love I met last summer
on the beach. But when anything—object, cloth,
or hands—come in contact, the beehive stirs,
then stings from my hairline down to my toes.
For months, you know, I slept in my clothes,
the thought of a dress brushing over my back too much.
The buzzing began in my ears even before I'd lie down,
then it'd come of its own with each toss or turn.
I'd wake up burning. The flames rising.
This little bell became my trail to the outside world.
Remember that trip to Tibet when we bought it

at the monastery, the monks' chants echoing down the valley?
I'd ring and you'd come to calm my screams and bring
a glass of water. We had no idea what was the matter,
and all the money Mother and Father left us
couldn't find a cause or cure. "Normal. Nothing unusual
shows up here. We could do further tests, but I suggest
you go home, rest, and try to eliminate stress."
Bells of Chartre, the Seville Cathedral,
Bell of St. Patrick's Will, harness bells
tinkling through the Moscow snow. I'd imagine myself
wrapped in a blanket of ice and dream of those monks
controlling their body temperature by breathing.
On the freezing mountain tops. Out, in.
I became a buoy at sea and most steered clear,
not knowing what to do, to say, thinking all along
I must be cracked. But we kept searching and you,
my dear, never let me drift. We tried a dry climate
and moved to the Texas desert, but there
the bees became scorpions and brown recluse spiders
eating holes through my pores. Here, the doctors
are trying to dig down and uncover the seed
of the problem and they have a hunch it may be
in my own mouth: mercury poisoning from the
dental amalgam. Tomorrow all my fillings will be
replaced with porcelain. My tongue moves from
side to side tolling the hours until it's time,
while outside the window over the lake, the sun
burns itself out. This morning while you were sleeping,
there was a code across the hall. I don't know
any of the details but through the door I saw
the swarms of teams, heard the elevator ding
when they rolled her away on the stretcher.
Sister, tonight I'll try to tolerate a sheet.
Let's pull it up toward my chin and then

I'd like you to cup your hands near my face,
ever so lightly, gently, as if you were reaching out
to pluck a piece of fruit ripe from a limb.

House of Cards

King of spades, ace of clubs,
as a kid, I stacked cards like this,
one by one, beams balanced in air.
I sat on the porch of our cabin
at the lake and placed my bets
against a breeze. Dragonfly days
were best—warm and still—
when the hovering of the insects'
wings over water was the only stir.

Then I learned that all things
take up space, share shape
and form, and if you build
a certain way—jack of diamonds
placed atop an eight of spades,
just right and not too far apart—
your house will hold together,
and all is shimmer and sheen:
the slick back of the deck,

bulging heads and eyes,
the slim bodies of the demoiselles,
the long arc of the walleye's neck
as it struggles free of the hook,
its scales metallic and glistening
in the sun. The same principles
apply every time—you work
from the inside out, the entrails
the essentials. You must choose

the best materials, wood, metal,
dirt, and bring what you know
of nature to your design.
For mine, glass, glass, glass.
The calm surface of that lake,
water and sand, stood on end
to surround even the most urban
building in the coolness of the clouds,
its body wading into the eddies
and coves, the lap and pull of
the skyline. We all want
to get out from behind walls,

to become part of the horizon,
but ten of spades, nine of clubs,
we find ourselves confined to wards
and rooms where the windows
are small and look out on other
narrow views, the late summer sunset

reduced to a glint concealed in
a concrete block. We all want
to go under, and feel the brush
of moss, of minnows against
our skin, to open our eyes
to the blur of water, of a pebble
drifting down to the bottom,
the mud cushioning its arrival,
the mud, a palm, a place to land.

We all wish our own
lungs could hold more mystery,
that the universe could flow through
without thought of breath or strokes,

just the current, the swirl,
our bones, flesh, guts, floating
as one and then finally—
queen of hearts, queen of clubs,
the welcoming, welcoming of the wind.

A NOTE ABOUT THE AUTHOR

Mary Swander is the author of two earlier books of poems, *Succession* (1979) and *Driving the Body Back* (1986). She has published a variety of writing widely, in such magazines as *The Nation, The New Yorker,* and *Poetry.* Her dramatic adaptation of *Driving the Body Back,* and her co-authored musical *Dear Iowa,* have been produced throughout the Midwest and on Iowa Public Television. She received her Master of Fine Arts degree from the University of Iowa Writer's Workshop, and she has been the recipient of a number of grants and awards, including one from the National Endowment for the Arts, the Literary Arts Award from the Chicago Public Library, and the *Nation*-Discovery Award. She is a native Iowan and an associate professor at Iowa State University. As an avid gardener, she has written for *National Gardening Magazine,* and is the co-author (with Jane Staw) of a book of interviews with midwestern gardeners, *Parsnips in the Snow* (1990).

A NOTE ON THE TYPE

The text of this book was set on the Linotype in a face called Primer, designed by the distinguished artist and engraver, Rudolph Ruzicka (1883–1978). It was first made generally available in 1954, although the design had been conceived some years before that, in answer to a request by Linotype that Ruzicka make a new version of a characterless but serviceable face called Century. This handsome design is the result.

Rudolph Ruzicka was born in what was then Bohemia, and came to America in 1894. He designed and illustrated many books (including a number for Alfred A. Knopf) and was the creator of a considerable list of individual prints in a variety of techniques. He was responsible for another widely used typeface called Fairfield.

Composition by Heritage Printers, Inc.,
Charlotte, North Carolina
Printed and bound by
Arcata Graphics/Kingsport,
Kingsport, Tennessee
Designed by Harry Ford